THE
MEDITERRANEAN
INSTANT POT COOKBOOK

EASY, HEALTHY & FLAVORFUL INSTANT POT RECIPES

FOR EATING WELL EVERY DAY

JENNIFER AUSTIN

Read4YourSelf Press

755 Pennsylvania Ave

San Francisco, CA 94107, USA

Ordering Information:

Quantity sales. Special discounts are available on quantity purchases by corporations, associations, and others. For details, contact the publisher at the address above.

Printed in the United States of America

Publisher's Cataloging-in-Publication data

1. The main category of the book — Mediterranean Cooking, Food & Wine

2. Another subject category — Weight Loss Diets (Books)

3. More categories — Weight Loss Recipes

First Edition- April 2020

Contents

Why Mediterranean Diet?

The Mediterranean diet is one of the healthiest dietary patterns for the prevention of cardiovascular diseases, hypertension, diabetes and cancer. The results of the PREDIMED study[1], in which researchers from the Balearic Islands participate, have shown that it is associated with greater life expectancy.

In the United States, where obesity is a public health problem, they have incorporated the Mediterranean diet pattern into the new dietary guidelines[2] based on the conclusions of the PREDIMED study.

With thousands of years, the Mediterranean Diet has been developed, with seasonal products, with different flavors and wines.

Mediterranean diet, was formed for centuries, on the shores of the Mediterranean Sea, countries were born, with diverse cultures, feeding on agriculture, fishing, hunting and livestock. The geographical area covers the Mediterranean Sea, with different altitudes, different seasonal and different foods, especially fruits and vegetables, which are subject to the collection time.

The Mediterranean diet is a healthy eating option, due to the variety and consumption of products of plant origin, its vitamin richness, the contribution of cereals and virgin olive oil.

All this is decisive and, in particular, the pressure cooker will be a great help to cook with energy efficiency.

The following aspects of the diet mark the characteristics of it.

Preferred consumption of:

- ✓ Fruits
- ✓ Vegetables
- ✓ Cereals, especially bread
- ✓ Fish
- ✓ Legumes
- ✓ Olive oil as the main source of fat

Low consumption of:

- ✓ Meat and meat products

Moderate consumption of:

- ✓ Dairy products; preferably skim, semi skim, fermented milk

The most important value of the Mediterranean diet is olive oil, rich in oleic acid and other components. It has a beneficial effect on health, preventing the development of coronary heart disease, cholesterol control and preventing some types of cancer, in addition to being a potent antioxidant, among other benefits. Its use is recommended as the main fat for dressings and fried foods.

[1] Estruch R, Ros E, Salas-Salvadó J, Covas MI, Corella D, Arós F, Gómez-Gracia E, Ruiz-Gutiérrez V, Fiol M, Lapetra J, Lamuela-Raventos RM. Primary prevention of cardiovascular disease with a Mediterranean diet. New England Journal of Medicine. 2013 Apr 4;368(14):1279-90.
[2] (2015- 2020 Dietary Guidelines for Americans)

6 Tips for success

There are many types of pressure-operated pots, from the classic ones with a valve on the lid that allows controlled steam escape as soon as there is a boil, to the quick-or-express pots, which have no steam outlet on the lid, but a valve that indicates the level of pressure inside. Whatever your model, it is very important to handle these pots carefully. If you have never used one, it is essential to read the manufacturer's instructions well.

Tip #1: Measure times

The cooking time in this type of containers is counted from the moment the pot has pressure and the rings rise, or pressure starts to flow out of the lid valve (depending on the model). The time difference between one and the other is usually almost double in the traditional one than in the fast one.

Tip #2: Remove the lid

It is very important to never open the pot when it has pressure. When you want to do it, remove the pot from the fire, wait for the rings to go down (or stop steam coming out of the valve) and the safety mechanism can be removed easily and without resistance. It is crucial: if you notice that it costs a little to open it, it is better to wait a few minutes. The difficulty is usually indicative that there is pressure inside and, therefore, steam and broth at a very high temperature.

Tip #3: Lower the pressure

If you want to lower the pressure quickly (at the risk of not having the recipe with the necessary rest) you can put the hot pot inside the sink and cool it under the cold water tap. By lowering the temperature, it will lose pressure more quickly.

Tip #4: Close the pot

In addition to making sure that the lid is properly placed, it is important to know when to close the pot. For example, when preparing legumes (which at the beginning of cooking usually release some impurities in the form of foam) it is advisable to close once the ingredients have begun to boil. This will allow you to remove these impurities with a slotted spoon and thus prevent them from clogging the valves of the pot inside.

Tip #5: Calculate the water

For cooking food we must follow the steps set by the recipe, with the following considerations:

- ✓ In sauteed and sauteed sausages you don't need much water to cook.

- ✓ In the case of vegetables or pureed vegetables, the volume of water you add should never exceed two-thirds of the pot's capacity because the juices can flow out of the valves once cooking begins.

- ✓ In soaking legumes, water should cover them until they are about five centimeters above.

- ✓ In stewed meat and vegetable stews with a little broth and a touch of wine, the water should be about two centimeters below the ingredients, since these will then release their juices during cooking.

Tip #6: Get a result similar to slow cooking

It is one of the biggest concerns and also one of the easiest to solve. So that the stews and vegetable dishes are almost the same as simmering in the traditional pot, just add ten more minutes of cooking, and with the pot open. So, once the indicated cooking time has elapsed, the pressure has dropped and the lid has been removed, take the fire for ten minutes so that the juices evaporate and the sauce or the broth is more bound.

Troubleshooting

Cooking rice and grains

The dry grain of cereals and other similar foods justifies the use of the pressure cooker since traditional cooking can take a long time. If there are indications in the package, reduce the normal cooking times by half. If there are no indications, cooking can be a big problem for you. For this reason, we will give you below how to solve those problems. We suggest these times for a cup of dry cereal, always referred to when the high pressure in the pot begins:

- ✓ Amaranth: between 3 and 8 minutes, with 470 ml of liquid.

- ✓ Wild rice: between 22 and 28 minutes, for 600 ml of liquid.

- ✓ Oat flakes: 2-6 minutes, for 600 ml.

- ✓ Oat grain: 20-22 minutes, in 470 ml.

- ✓ Pearl barley: 18-22 minutes, in 600 ml.

- ✓ Barley grain: 25 minutes, 700 ml.

- ✓ Black barley: 25 minutes, 700 ml.

- ✓ Rye in grain (soaked): 25 minutes, with 350-470 ml.

- ✓ Spelled (soaked): 22 minutes, 350 ml.

- ✓ Whole Farro (soaked): 6-7 minutes, between 470 and 590 ml.

- ✓ Match freekeh: 7-8 minutes, in 350 ml.

- ✓ Kamut (soaked): 10-15 minutes, in 470 ml.

- ✓ Millet: 10 minutes, 415 ml.

- ✓ Quinoa: 10 minutes, 400 ml.

- ✓ Sorghum: 30-35 minutes, 600 ml.

- ✓ Teff: 3 minutes, 600 ml.

- ✓ Whole wheat (soaked): 10-15 minutes, 470 ml.

- ✓ Buckwheat: 3 minutes, 400 ml.

- ✓ Triticale (soaked): 20 minutes, 470 m

Cooking must be done with medium heat since the grain does not have a strong fire. If you see that these times are insufficient, return the pot to the pressure fire for one or two minutes. You can go checking until you reach the ideal point.

Soak or not? Soaking is convenient before cooking when the grain is especially hard.

So, if you don't want to soak, simply add 10 minutes of cooking to the indicated times.

Cooking beans and lentils

- ❖ _Beans_

Check the beans. Those that are broken, take them off. We also recommend giving them a first bath so they don't have dirt.

In a pot, pour the beans with enough water to cover them and one more finger. Let them soak between one hour and one night; the longer, the better the result.

- ❖ _Lentils_

In the case of lentils, prepare them with cold water, while chickpeas in hot water so that they are not hard. Over high heat for 10 minutes and then lower it.

To accelerate even more place a spoonful of bicarbonate per liter of water.

Cooking vegetables

Pressure cooking vegetables that cook very quickly requires precision: use the mobile's stopwatch.

In many recipes that have several kinds of vegetables, those that are made faster are simply introduced into the pot, raw, when we have depressurized them to cook them with the residual heat. In some cases, the vegetable gets into the pot, the pot is covered and so it is done alone for a few minutes.

If you have a pot with two positions, high pressure (2) and low (1), the low pressure allows cooking the vegetable twice as long as the high, so you can be more precise. Above all, use it with peas, bok choy, broccoli or summer squashes -which are pumpkins, but more immature. Anyway, the total time will not be much, so do not leave the kitchen unattended.

Measurement Conversations and equivalents

Recipes Measurements	USA to the Metric System
Measurement Equivalences For Cooking 1 tablespoon = 3 teaspoons 1/16 cup = 1 tablespoon 1/8 cup = 2 tablespoons 1/6 cup = 2 + 2 teaspoons 1/4 cup = 4 tablespoons 1/3 cup = 5 + 1 teaspoon 3/8 cup = 6 tablespoons 1/2 cup = 8 tablespoons 2/3 cup = 10 + 2 tablespoons 3/4 cup = 12 tablespoons 1 cup = 16 tablespoons 1 cup = 48 teaspoons 1 cup = 8 fluid ounces 2 cups = 1 pint 2 pints = 1 quart 4 cups = 1 quart 1 inch (in) = 2.54 centimeters (cm) 16 ounces (oz) = 1 pound	To Convert Fluids 1/5 teaspoon = 1 ml 1 teaspoon = 5 ml 1 tablespoon = 15 ml 1 fluid ounces = 30 ml 1/5 cup = 50 ml 1 cup = 240 ml 2 cups (1 pint) = 470 ml 4 cups (1 quart) = .95 liter 4 quarts (1 gal.) = 3.8 liters

To Convert Weight	Abbreviations For Fluid Measurement	Abbreviations For Weight Measurement
1 oz. = 28 grams 1 pound = 454 grams	ml means milliliter cc is the same as ml ounce - means fluid ounces gal. means gallon	g means grams lbs means pounds oz - means ounce (Weight)

Metric System to USA	Weight
To Convert Fluids 1 milliliter = 1/5 teaspoon 5 ml = 1 teaspoon 15 ml = 1 tablespoon 30 ml = 1 fluid ounce 47 ml = 1/5 cup 100 ml = 3.4 fluid ounces 237 ml = 1 cup 240 ml = 1 cup 473 ml = 2 cups .95 liter = 4 cups 3.8 liters = 4 quarts (1 gal.) 1 liter = 34 fluid ounces 1 liter = 4.2 cups 1 liter = 2.1 pints	1 gram = .035 ounce 100 grams = 3.5 ounces 500 grams = 1.10 pounds 1 kilogram = 2,205 pounds 1 kilogram = 35 ounce

Chapter 1

Breakfast and Brunch

Apple Pie Oatmeal

Servings: 4

Calories: 481

Preparation time: 2 minutes

Cook time: 8 minutes

Ingredients	Steps to Cook

Ingredients

- 1 tbsp salted butter
- 1 glass oatmeal cut
- 2 cups water
- ½ glass of apple cider
- 2 tbsp brown sugar1 teaspoon cinnamon
- 1 large apple, peeled and heartless, diced
- Fresh whipped cream nuts and diced apple

Steps to Cook

1. Configure your instant pot to saute and add butter. Allow the butter to melt, spreading it across the bottom of the instant pot.
2. Add the oatmeal and stir to cover the butter.
3. Stir continuously for about 2 minutes or until the oatmeal begins to toast.
4. Pour water, cider, brown sugar, cinnamon and apple. Stir to combine. Change the instant pot to "pressure cooking" and adjust for 8 minutes.
5. When finished cooking, let stand for 5 minutes, naturally releasing part of the steam. Then press the release and allow the remaining steam to leave the pot.
6. Open the pot (be careful!) and stir to cool the oatmeal.

Quinoa And Cheese Breakfast

Servings: 6

Calories: 244.2

Preparation time: 5 minutes

Cook time: 8 minutes

Ingredients

- 8 eggs
- 2 cups cooked quinoa
- ½ cup green pepper
- ½ cup red pepper, diced
- ½ cup diced tomato
- ¼ cup diced onion
- 2 tablespoons soy sauce
- 6 ounces grated panela cheese
- 1 medium avocado, diced
- ¼ cup chopped cilantro
- Oil spray
- Salt to taste

Steps to Cook

1. In a bowl, beat the eggs. Reserve.
2. Spray the spray oil in the pot, and preheat at medium-high temperature for about 3 minutes.
3. Reduce the temperature to medium. Add all vegetables, with the exception of avocado and cilantro. Sauté for 1 minute, while stirring constantly.
4. Spray a little more oil and add the beaten eggs. Stir with the Silicone Spatula, until the egg is well cooked (in about 4 minutes). Add cooked quinoa and soy sauce, and cook for 1minute more. Remove from the pot.
5. Add the cheese, cover and let stand for about 2 minutes.
6. Serve immediately with avocado and decorate with the chopped cilantro.

Vegetable Soup

Servings: 3

Calories: 80

Preparation time: 5 minutes

Cook time: 5 minutes

Ingredients

- 28ml white or black beans
- 2 tablespoons chickpeas
- 1 onion
- 2 carrots
- 2 potatoes
- 2 turnips
- 1 sprig of celery
- Some cabbage leaves
- A handful of peas
- Broccoli

Steps to Cook

1. The vegetables were soaked the night before.
2. The pot is filled with 1 liter of cold water and when it starts to boil, all the ingredients are added except the salt and close the instant pot.
3. Vegetables are peeled and cut into large pieces. After a very short time, the cooking indicator will rise, keep it in the second ring for 8 minutes.
4. Open the pot, once you have ensured that all the pressure in the pot has been removed. Pass the broth through a sieve. Once strained, check the salt point.
5. It can be served alone or with pasta noodles.
6. You can also beat an egg and add it to the broth at the last moment, beating without stopping. With vegetables and legumes, you can prepare a puree or take them apart with olive oil.

Steamed Salmon In A Pressure Cooker

Servings: 4

Calories: 170

Preparation time: 2 minutes

Cook time: 5 minutes

Ingredients

- 450g of salmon
- 236ml of water
- 2 sprigs of rosemary
- 5ml mustard powder
- Salt and pepper to taste

Steps to Cook

1. The vegetables were soaked the night before.
2. Pour water into the optimal instant pot and place the steam grill correctly inside.
3. Put the salmon on the rack and season with rosemary, mustard powder, pepper and salt to taste. Cover the instant pot, remove the weight and simmer for 5 minutes. After 5 minutes, turn off the heat, remove the lid carefully and serve immediately.

Apple, Cinnamon And Oatmeal

Servings: 2

Calories: 160

Preparation time: 3 min

Cook time: 12 minutes

Ingredients

- 2 tbsp unsalted butter
- 1 ½ cups oatmeal cut in steel
- 4 ½ cups of water
- 1 large apple peeled and diced
- ¼ cup brown sugar or maple syrup
- 1 tsp ground cinnamon
- ¾ teaspoon salt
- Brown sugar
- ¾ cup roasted and chopped walnuts

Steps to Cook

1. Select the Sauté setting in your instant pot cooker and melt the butter. Add the oatmeal and cook, stirring frequently, for about 5 minutes, until the oatmeal is aromatic and lightly toasted. Add water, apple, brown sugar, cinnamon and salt to oatmeal, making sure all oats are submerged in the liquid.
2. Secure the instant pot lid. Cancel the Sauté program, and set the cooking time for 12 minutes at high pressure.
3. When the cooking program is finished, allow the pressure to release naturally for at least 10 minutes, then move the pressure relief to Ventilation to release the remaining steam. Open the pot and stir the oatmeal to incorporate any extra liquid. Serve the oatmeal in bowls and cover with butter, brown sugar and chopped nuts.

Oatmeal Gruel

Servings: 2

Calories: 389

Preparation time: 1 minute

Cook time: 2 minutes

Ingredients

- 2 cups whole oatmeal
- 3 liters fresh milk
- 1 can condensed milk
- 1 large slice of cinnamon

Steps to Cook

1. Gather the ingredients.
2. If you have a pressure cooker, put all the ingredients, stir, cover and simmer, so that it does not stick. If not, no problem, use the pot you have, only you need to constantly shake, because it can be pasted. You only need to boil for about 2 minutes.

Wholemeal Porridge

Servings: 4

Calories: 389

Preparation time: 5 minute

Cook time: 50 minutes

Ingredients

- 1 cup of 175 grams of whole oats
- A pinch of sea salt

Steps to Cook

1. Wash the oatmeal and let it soak in six cups (liter and a half) of water for six hours, or overnight.
2. Put the oatmeal in the instant pot with salt and bring it to a pressure point. Put the pot on a flame diffuser, reduce the heat to a minimum and let it cook for about 50 minutes.
3. Another way to cook it is by heating the oatmeal very slowly in a cast iron pan, for several hours, stirring occasionally.

Chapter 2
Poultries

Laurel Leaf Chicken

Servings: 4

Calories: 253

Preparation time: 5 minute

Cook time: 4h

Ingredients	Steps to Cook

Ingredients

- 1 ½ to 2 pounds boneless skinless chicken breasts or thighs
- 1 cup of water
- 1 teaspoon of salt (use less if chicken is in brine or previously seasoned)
- 2 bay leaves
- 3 garlic cloves

Steps to Cook

1. Arrange the chicken in a single uniform layer at the bottom of the pressure cooker. Add the water, then sprinkle with salt. Add the bay leaves and garlic.
2. Make sure the pressure regulator is in the "Sealed" position. Select the "Pressure Cooker" or "Manual" program, then set the time to 10 minutes at high pressure. It will take about 10 minutes for the pressure cooker to reach maximum pressure. Cooking time begins once maximum pressure has been reached.
3. As soon as the timer goes off at the end of cooking, perform a quick pressure release by moving the pressure release knob from "Sealed" to "Vent".

Oriental Chicken Wings

Servings: 4
Calories: 160
Preparation time: 5 minute
Cook time: 30 minutes

Ingredients

- 800 g of chicken wings
- 1 tablespoon of honey
- 1 lime
- 50 ml of soy sauce
- 3-4 slices of fresh ginger
- 1 teaspoon of instant starch thickener
- Black pepper
- 2 thin chives
- Fresh chives
- Fresh coriander

Steps to Cook

1. Remove the tip of the wings. Split the wings in two at the joint of the joint. Mix the honey, soy sauce, lime zest and its juice, pepper and ginger to make the marinade.
2. Put the wings in a zip bag and pour the marinade liquid inside.
3. Store the bag cold for 8 hours. Move the bag to redistribute the liquid. Open the bag and place the wings in the Instant Pot. Brush the wings with part of the marinade and discard the remaining liquid that is left in the bag. Sprinkle a teaspoon of instant starch thickener on the wings. Cook for 30 minutes on HIGH.
4. Clean the chive, remove the driest layers and cut it into slices. Chop the chives very finely and separate the coriander leaves from the stems.
5. Collect the juice from the wings and transfer it to a saucepan. Reduce the heat until it is somewhat thick.

Instant Pot Chicken and Rice

Servings: 4

Calories: 283

Preparation time: 10 minute

Cook time: 10 minutes

Ingredients

- 1 pound sliced fresh mushrooms
- 1/2 chopped onion
- 1 cup long-grain white rice
- 3 chicken breasts, 7-8 ounces each
- 1 3/4 cups low-sodium chicken stock or water
- 10 ounces condensed mushroom cream
- salt and black pepper

Steps to Cook

1. Grease in a 6QT instant pot. Season the chicken breasts with salt and pepper to taste. Rinse the rice with cold water until the water runs clear.
2. Add mushrooms, onion, rice, chicken breasts to the instant pot. Pour the broth over the chicken breasts. Spread the mushroom soup on top of the chicken breasts. Do not stir. Put the instant pot in MANUAL. Choose HIGH PRESSURE for 10 minutes.
3. Once complete, let Instant Pot release naturally for 10 minutes. Release any remaining pressure.
4. Open the Instant Pot and remove the chicken. Stir in the rice and mushrooms. Shred the chicken and put the rice back and mix well.
5. Garnish with parsley if desired and serve.

Chicken With Soy Sauce

Servings: 4

Calories: 169

Preparation time: 5 minute

Cook time: 5 minutes

Ingredients

- 4 boneless chicken breasts, skinless, in halves
- ½ cup of water
- ¼ cup low-calorie soy sauce
- ½ cup sliced mushrooms
- ½ sliced onion
- ½ cup sliced celery
- 3 tablespoons brown sugar

Steps to Cook

1. Put all the ingredients in the pot. Close and secure the lid.
2. Place the pressure regulator on the vent tube and cook 4 minutes once the pressure regulator begins to rock slowly.
3. Let the pressure decrease on its own.

Chicken With Chutney Sauce

Servings: 6

Calories: 258

Preparation time: 5 minute

Cook time: 4 minutes

Ingredients

- 6 boneless chicken breasts, skinless, in halves
- 15 ounce tomatoes
- 1 4-ounce can chopped green chili peppers
- 1 tbsp vinegar
- 1 tbsp brown sugar
- ¼ tsp allspice
- ¼ cup of water
- 1 tbsp cornstarch
- ½ cup raisins
- ½ cup mango chutney sauce

Steps to Cook

1. Put all the ingredients in the pot, except water and cornstarch.
2. Close and secure the lid. Place the pressure regulator on the vent tube and cook 4 minutes once the pressure regulator begins to rock slowly.
3. Let the pressure decrease on its own. Remove the chicken and keep it warm. Mix the water with the cornstarch.
4. Add the sauce and stir. Heat until the sauce thickens, stirring constantly.

Chicken With Herbs

Servings: 6

Calories: 250

Preparation time: 5 minute

Cook time: 8 minutes

Ingredients

- 1 tbsp vegetable oil
- 1 cup chopped onion
- 1 tbsp minced garlic
- 3 pounds of chicken thighs, skinless
- 1 cup chicken broth
- 1 tbsp chopped parsley
- ½ cup celery leaves
- 1 tsp oregano
- 1 tsp basil
- 4 ounces black olives
- 2 tbsp cold water
- 2 tbsp flour
- Salt and pepper to taste

Steps to Cook

1. Pour oil into the pot. Sauté the onions and garlic over medium heat. Remove from heat. Brown the chicken. Add onion, garlic, broth, parsley, celery leaves, oregano and basil. Close and secure the lid.
2. Place the pressure regulator on the vent tube and cook 8 minutes once the pressure regulator begins to rock slowly. Cool the pot quickly. Remove the chicken and place it on a hot serving plate.
3. Add the olives to the liquid and heat. Mix the water with the flour. Add to hot broth and stir. Heat until the sauce thickens, stirring constantly. Pour the sauce over the chicken.

Biryani Chicken With Brown Rice

Servings: 1
Calories: 390
Preparation time: 8 minute
Cook time: 17 minutes

Ingredients

- 1 teaspoon olive oil
- 1 medium onion, chopped
- 2 cloves garlic, minced
- ½ cup brown rice
- ½ chicken breasts, skin and visible fat removed
- ¾ cup diced tomatoes dried herbs of your choice
- 1 cup chicken broth (optional)
- Salt and pepper to taste

Steps to Cook

1. Heat the olive oil and sauté the onion and garlic. Add the rice and stir.
2. Fry until the rice becomes aromatic and begins to turn brown. Add chicken previously seasoning, tomatoes, chicken/water broth, salt, herbs and pepper.
3. Bring to a boil, then simmer over low heat, tightly covered, until fully cooked.

California Chicken

Servings: 6

Calories: 291

Preparation time: 5 minute

Cook time: 4 minutes

Ingredients

- 2 tablespoons vegetable oil
- 6 boneless chicken breasts, skinless, in halves
- 1 teaspoon rosemary
- 3 cloves garlic, peeled and sliced
- ½ cup white wine
- ½ cup chicken broth
- ¼ cup chopped parsley
- ½ lemon, finely sliced
- Salt and pepper to taste

Steps to Cook

1. Pour oil into the pot. Brown the chicken in the pressure cooker over medium heat.
2. Season the chicken with the rosemary. Cover the chicken with the garlic.
3. Mix the wine, broth and parsley; pour them over the chicken. Close and secure the lid.
4. Place the pressure regulator on the vent tube and cook 4 minutes once the pressure regulator begins to rock slowly.
5. Cool the pot quickly. Garnish the chicken with the lemon slices.

Stuffed Jalapeno

Servings: 8-10

Calories: 110.7

Preparation time: 5 minute

Cook time: 20 minutes

Ingredients

- 1 pound (½ kg) ground chicken
- 1 teaspoon finely chopped garlic
- 16 medium jalapeños cut in half (without seeds)
- 1½ cups ricotta cheese
- 32 slices of turkey bacon
- Toothpicks / Wooden sticks (toothpicks)

Steps to Cook

1. Preheat the pot to 350 ° F. Add the chicken with the garlic, and cook for 4 minutes, while stirring constantly. Transfer the chicken to the 3-quart Mixing Bowl, and set aside.
2. Add the jalapeños to the same pan and cook them for 5 minutes, while stirring constantly. Remove and reserve.
3. Stir the chicken with ricotta cheese.
4. Fill the 32 halves of jalapeño with the chicken mixture, and roll them well with the turkey bacon. Secure them with wooden sticks.
5. Place the stuffed jalapeños in the pot, cover and cook for 10 minutes at 280°F. If they are very large, cook one half first and then the other.
6. Let cool a couple of minutes and enjoy.

Bittersweet Chicken

Servings: 6

Calories: 333

Preparation time: 5 minute

Cook time: 8 minutes

Ingredients

- 1 tbsp vegetable oil
- 3 pounds chicken
- 1 8-ounce pineapple
- ½ cup sliced celery
- 1 red chili pepper
- ¼ cup brown sugar
- ½ cup vinegar
- 2 tbsp soy sauce
- 1 tbsp of ketchup
- ½ teaspoon Worcestershire sauce
- ¼ tsp ground ginger
- 2 tbsp cold water
- 2 tbsp cornstarch

Steps to Cook

1. Pour oil into the pot. Brown the chicken in the Instant Pot over medium heat. Combine the remaining ingredients, less water and cornstarch, in a separate bowl. Pour them over the chicken. Close and secure the lid.
2. Place the pressure regulator on the vent tube and cook 8 minutes once the pressure regulator begins to rock slowly. Cool the pot quickly.
3. Remove chicken, pineapple and vegetables, and place them on a hot serving plate. Mix the water with the cornstarch.
4. Add to hot liquid and stir. Heat until the sauce thickens, stirring constantly.
5. Pour the sauce over chicken, pineapple and vegetables.

Cacciatore Chicken

Servings: 6
Calories: 291
Preparation time: 5 minute
Cook time: 8 minutes

Ingredients

- 3 pounds of chicken serving portions
- 1 cup diced tomatoes
- ⅓ cup white wine
- 1½ cups sliced onions
- ½ cup chopped carrots
- ½ cup chopped celery
- 2 cloves garlic, minced
- 2 tbsp chopped parsley
- 1 teaspoon oregano
- 1 teaspoon salt
- ¼ tsp black pepper
- 1 can of 6 ounces of tomato extract

Steps to Cook

1. Pour oil into the pot. Brown the chicken in the Instant.
2. Put all the ingredients, except the tomato extract, in the pressure cooker.
3. Close and secure the lid. Place the pressure regulator on the vent tube and cook 8 minutes once the pressure regulator begins to rock slowly.
4. Cool the pot quickly. Put the chicken on a hot serving plate.
5. Add the tomato extract to the sauce in the pot and stir.
6. Cook over low heat until it thickens. Pour over chicken.

Stewed Chicken

Servings: 2-4

Calories: 222

Preparation time: 5 minute

Cook time: 15 minutes

Ingredients

- 1 pound chicken
- 3 tablespoons oil
- 1 onion
- 2 cloves garlic
- 1 tomato
- 1 carrot
- ½ kg peas
- 4 artichokes
- 2 potatoes
- salt and pepper
- 1 cup water

Steps to Cook

1. Cut the chicken into pieces or small pieces, as if to cook. Sauté in oil, remove the chicken and in the same oil brown the well-chopped onion and garlic.
2. When the onion turns brown, add the tomato (skinless and seedless).
3. Then the sliced carrot, the quartered artichokes, the peas and the quartered potatoes as well.
4. Season the chicken, add to the pot and pour the water, close the pot, cook under pressure for 15 minutes. It is served with boiled eggs cut into slices. Very rich..

Tlalpeño Broth

Servings: 8

Calories: 367

Preparation time: 5 minute

Cook time: 45 minutes

Ingredients

- 4 pounds skinless chicken
- Salt and pepper
- 6 cups chickpeas
- 1 cup carrots, sliced
- ½ cup onion, diced
- ¼ cup cilantro
- 2 cloves garlic
- 3 chipotle peppers
- 10 cups of water
- Garrison:
- 1 avocado, sliced
- 4 radishes, sliced
- Tortillas in strips
- Lemon slices

Steps to Cook

1. In the pressure cooker, add the chicken, previously seasoned with salt and black pepper, and the rest of the ingredients. Do not fill the unit more than two thirds of its capacity.

2. Cover, close and cook at medium-high temperature. Once the throttle valve whistles and releases steam (in approximately 12 to 15 minutes), reduce the temperature to medium and cook for 30 minutes. Make sure the regulator has released steam before continuing cooking.

3. Turn off the burner, turn the regulator valve indicator to the pressure release icon, and allow all steam to be released before opening the lid. The correct way to know is when the red indicator goes down. Make sure the chickpeas are well cooked. If necessary, add salt and black pepper to taste.

Bayou Bounty Chicken

Servings: 3
Calories: 394
Preparation time: 5 minute
Cook time: 5 minutes

Ingredients

- 1½ pounds of chicken pieces
- 1 can of 15 ounces whole tomatoes, cut
- ¾ cup chopped onion
- ⅓ cup chopped green pepper
- ⅓ cup chopped celery
- 2 cloves garlic, minced
- ½ tablespoon extra spicy seasoning mix
- Hot cooked rice

Steps to Cook

1. Put all ingredients, except rice, in the Instant Pot. Close and secure the lid. Place the pressure regulator on the vent tube and cook 8 minutes once the pressure regulator begins to rock slowly.
2. Let the pressure decrease on its own. Serve chicken and sauce over rice.

Tarragon Chicken Breasts

Servings: 4

Calories: 219

Preparation time: 5 minute

Cook time: 10 minutes

Ingredients

- 1 tbsp vegetable oil
- 4 boneless chicken breasts
- ½ cup Worcestershire sauce with white wine
- ½ cup white wine
- ¼ cup chopped onion
- ¼ cup sliced celery
- ¼ cup sliced carrots
- 1 tsp tarragon
- 1 tsp salt
- ¼ tsp black pepper
- ¼ cup cold water
- 1 tbsp cornstarch

Steps to Cook

1. Pour oil into the pot. Brown the chicken in the Instant Pot over medium heat. Add the remaining ingredients, less water and cornstarch.
2. Close and secure the lid. Place the pressure regulator on the vent tube and cook 4 minutes once the pressure regulator begins to rock slowly.
3. Cool the pot quickly. Remove the chicken and keep it warm. Mix the water with the cornstarch. Add the sauce and stir.
4. Heat until the sauce thickens, stirring constantly.

White Pozole

Servings: 4

Calories: 223.1

Preparation time: 5 minute

Cook time: 35 minutes

Ingredients

- 1 pork loin cut
- 1 teaspoon of corn oil
- 1 tsp of oregano
- 1 teaspoon of cumin
- Chicken power broth
- 3 bay leaves
- 4 cups peanut
- 4 cups chicken broth
- 2 cups of water
- 1 cup green sauce
- 1 cup sliced red radishes
- 1 cup red onion
- 4 cups lettuce
- 2 lemons, cut into quarters

Steps to Cook

1. Cut the pork loin into pieces and season it with powdered chicken broth, oregano and cumin. In a skillet, add a little corn oil and brown the seasoned pork loin pieces. Add the golden pieces of pork tenderloin to the Instant Pot and pour four cups of chicken broth, 2 cups of water, one tablespoon of chicken broth powder, and precooked peanut butter.

2. Seal the Instant Pot making sure the valve is positioned correctly and choose the "Meat/Stew" cooking mode. It takes 35 minutes for the pork pozole to be ready in the instant pressure cooker. While the pork pozole is cooking, prepare the green nugget sauce. Toast the seeds together with the tomatillos, garlic and serranos. Blend until you get a thick sauce. Prepare the side dishes of the pork pozole by cleaning and cutting the red radishes, finely chopping a purple onion, finely slicing lettuce and cutting the lemons into quarters.

Chapter 3

Pork, Beef and Lamb

Pork Ribs

Servings: 4

Calories: 270

Preparation time: 5 minute

Cook time: 10 minutes

| Ingredients | Steps to Cook |

Ingredients

- 1.5 kg pork ribs
- 2 tbsp chopped garlic
- 1 tbsp soy sauce
- Salt and pepper
- 45 g of butter
- 30 ml of vegetable oil

For the sauce:

- 60 ml white wine
- 5 tbsp white sugar
- 1 tbsp cornstarch

Steps to Cook

1. Season the ribs and season with garlic and soy sauce, reserve in refrigeration. In a bowl mix the sauce ingredients and reserve. Heat the Instant Pot, melt the butter and add the vegetable oil. Seal the ribs with maceration on both sides.

2. Add the passion fruit sauce and cover by aligning the arrow on the pot handle with the arrow on the lid, place on the stove at high flame with the pressure regulator for 10 minutes until the safety valve is activated, lower the temperature to medium heat and cook for 30 minutes. Let cool to remove pressure..

Ground Beef And Spaghetti

Servings: 4

Calories: 229

Preparation time: 5 minute

Cook time: 20 minutes

Ingredients

- 1 tablespoon of olive oil
- 1 pound lean ground beef
- 1 small onion, chopped
- 3 garlic cloves, minced
- ¼ cup dry red wine *
- 1 sauce (25 ounces) marinara sauce
- 1 ¾ cups beef broth
- 8 ounces bluebell pasta
- Kosher salt and freshly ground black pepper, to taste.
- ¼ cup chopped fresh basil leaves
- 1/3 up freshly grated Parmesan cheese

Steps to Cook

1. Set a 6 qt Instant Pot® in the high stir fry setting. Heat the olive oil; add ground beef and cook until golden brown, about 3-5 minutes, making sure to shred the meat while cooking; drain excess fat.
2. Add onion and cook, stirring frequently, until translucent, about 2-3 minutes. Add garlic until fragrant, about 1 minute.
3. Add the wine, scraping up the golden pieces from the bottom of the pot.
4. Add marinara sauce, beef broth, and pasta; Season with salt and pepper to taste. Select manual configuration; Set the pressure to high and set the time to 5 minutes. When you finish cooking, quickly release the pressure according to the manufacturer's instructions. Add the basil and Parmesan cheese.
5. Serve immediately.

Casserole Beef

Servings: 6

Calories: 297

Preparation time: 5 minute

Cook time: 45 minutes

Ingredients

- 3 pounds of beef for casserole
- 1 tablespoon vegetable oil
- A carrot
- 2 cups of water
- Salt and pepper
- 1 small onion, chopped
- 1 bay leaf

Steps to Cook

1. Pour oil into the pot. Brown the beef on both sides in medium pressure over medium heat. Remove beef. Pour the water into the pot. Place the meat on the rack of the pot.
2. Put the meat with salt, pepper, onions and bay leaf. Close and secure the lid. Place the pressure regulator on the vent tube and cook 45 minutes once the pressure regulator begins to rock slowly.
3. Let the pressure decrease on its own. If desired, thicken the meat sauce.

Canned Bee

Servings: 6

Calories: 295

Preparation time: 5 minute

Cook time: 60 minutes

Ingredients	Steps to Cook

- 3 pounds of corned beef
- 2 cups of water
- 1 tablespoon garlic powder
- 1 bay leaf

1. Pour the water into the pot. Rub garlic powder on all surfaces of corned beef. Put the meat on the rack of the pot.
2. Add the bay leaf. Close and secure the lid. Place the pressure regulator on the vent tube and cook 60 minutes once the pressure regulator begins to rock slowly. Let the pressure decrease on its own.
3. Tip: If corned beef comes with a package of condiments, use it and skip the bay leaf.

Lamb Chops With Coffee

Servings: 6

Calories: 165

Preparation time: 5 minute

Cook time: 16 minutes

Ingredients

- 16 ounces (450 g) lamb chops
- ¼ cup ground espresso coffee
- 1 teaspoon chili powder
- 1 teaspoon ground cumin
- 1 teaspoon salt
- 1 teaspoon black pepper

Marsala sauce:

- ¼ cup marsala wine
- ¼ cup chicken broth
- ¼ cup double cream

Steps to Cook

1. In a bowl, stir the ground espresso, chili, cumin, salt and pepper. Pass the lamb chops through this mixture, and reserve them.
2. In the pot, mix all the sauce ingredients. Let reduce for about 7 minutes, at medium temperature, until it thickens a bit. Stir occasionally.
3. Preheat a skillet at medium-high temperature for 3 minutes, or until a few drops of water are sprayed, they bounce off the surface without evaporating. Place the chops and cook for 4 minutes with the lid ajar.
4. Turn them over, reduce the temperature to medium, and cook for 5 minutes with the lid ajar; remove them from the skillet. If you want them to be well cooked, let them cook for 2 more minutes.
5. Serve the chops and cover with the sauce.

Pork Chops With Apple

Servings: 4

Calories: 311.5

Preparation time: 5 minute

Cook time: 14 minutes

Ingredients

- 8 boneless pork chops (4 oz / 113 g each)
- 4 sliced red apples
- 2 teaspoons brown sugar
- ½ cup chopped walnuts
- ¼ cup maple syrup
- ¼ teaspoon ground nutmeg
- Salt and black pepper to taste

Steps to Cook

1. Pepper the pork chops. Preheat the pot at medium-high temperature for 3 minutes, or until a few drops of water are sprayed, they roll over the surface without evaporating. Add the chops and brown them for 4 minutes, with the lid ajar.
2. Flip the chops with the spatula and add the other ingredients.
3. Cover with the valve closed and cook at low temperature for 10 minutes.
4. Serve with mashed potatoes.

Sautéed Meat

Servings: 4

Calories: 245.5

Preparation time: 5 minute

Cook time: 11 minutes

Ingredients

- 1 pound (½ kg) beef tenderloin
- 1 teaspoon sesame oil
- 1 cup red pepper, cut into squares
- 1 cup green pepper, cut into squares
- 1 cup chopped broccoli
- ½ cup chopped green onion
- ½ cup purple onion
- ¾ cup beef broth
- ¼ cup soy sauce
- 1 tsp sesame seeds
- Salt and black pepper to taste

Steps to Cook

1. In a bowl, add the teaspoon of sesame oil and preheat the pot at medium-high temperature for about 3 minutes. Add the meat and cook for 3 minutes, while stirring constantly with the spatula.
2. Add the rest of the ingredients, except sesame seeds, beef broth and soy sauce. Saute for 3 more minutes.
3. Reduce heat to low, add beef broth and soy sauce, and cook for 5 minutes. Adjust the seasoning with salt and black pepper to taste. Sprinkle sesame seeds and serve with white rice.

Porcupine Meatballs

Servings: 4

Calories: 350

Preparation time: 5 minute

Cook time: 12 minutes

Ingredients

- 1 pound ground beef, fat free
- ⅓cup large uncooked white grain rice
- 2 tbsp tomato extract
- 1 teaspoon salt
- ¼ teaspoon of pepper
- ½ cup chopped onion
- ¼ cup sliced celery
- ¼ cup chopped green pepper
- 1 cup tomato sauce
- ½ cup of water
- 1 spoon of sugar
- ½ tsp dried mustard

Steps to Cook

1. Combine ground beef, rice, tomato extract, salt and pepper. Mix well. Form 8 meatballs. Place them in the pot.
2. Add the onion, celery and green pepper. Combine tomato paste, water, sugar and mustard.
3. Pour over meatballs. Close and secure the lid. Place the pressure regulator on the vent tube and cook 12 minutes once the pressure regulator begins to rock slowly. Cool the pot quickly.

Swiss Steak

Servings: 6

Calories: 251

Preparation time: 5 minute

Cook time: 18 minutes

Ingredients

- 2 pounds of hip steak, 1 inch thick
- 1 8-ounce can of tomato sauce
- ½ cup of water
- 1 cup chopped onion
- ½ cup chopped green pepper
- ½ cup sliced celery
- ½ teaspoon salt
- ¼ teaspoon of pepper

Steps to Cook

1. Put all the ingredients in the pot.
2. Close and secure the lid. Place the pressure regulator on the vent tube and cook 18 minutes once the pressure regulator begins to rock slowly.
3. Cool the pot quickly. If desired, thicken the sauce.

Stuffed Skirt Steak

Servings: 4
Calories: 237
Preparation time: 5 minute
Cook time: 18 minutes

Ingredients

- 1 tablespoon butter
- ½ cup chopped onion
- ½ cup chopped celery
- 1 clove of minced garlic
- 6 tbsp beef broth, divided
- 1 cup of breadcrumbs
- ½ teaspoon salt
- ¼ teaspoon marjoram
- ¼ teaspoon thyme
- ⅛ tsp black pepper
- 1 pound skirt steak, cut into 2 equal parts
- 1 can of 15 ounces chopped tomatoes

Steps to Cook

1. Add the butter to the pot. Sauté the onions, celery and garlic over medium heat.
2. Add 2 tablespoons of the broth, bread crumbs, salt, marjoram, thyme and pepper to the preparation.
3. Put the stuffing mixture on one of the steaks. Put the other steak on top. Hold with two toothpicks or metal skewers.
4. Place the steak in the pot, add the remaining 4 tablespoons of stock and the tomatoes and stir. Close and secure the lid.
5. Place the pressure regulator on the vent tube and cook 18 minutes once the pressure regulator begins to rock slowly. Let the pressure decrease on its own.
6. If desired, thicken the sauce.

Holiday Roast

Servings: 16-20

Calories: 75

Preparation time: 1h

Cook time: 30 minutes

Ingredients

- 12 pounds beef
- ½ cup finely chopped fresh thyme
- ½ cup finely chopped fresh rosemary
- 4 pounds potatoes
- 2 tbsp garlic
- ½ cup soy sauce
- 1½ cups beef broth
- ½ cup red wine
- 2 pounds carrots
- 1 pound of mushrooms
- 2 tsp fine cornmeal
- Salt and black pepper to taste

Steps to Cook

1. In a bowl, season the meat with thyme, rosemary, salt and black pepper. Cover and marinate for 15 minutes in the refrigerator. In a bowl, season the potatoes with garlic, salt and black pepper. In the other bowl, mix the soy sauce, beef broth and red wine; reserve.
2. Place the pan on the pot, and preheat at medium-high temperature for about 3 minutes. Add the meat and seal it for 16 minutes. Add the potatoes, carrots and the broth mixture. Reduce the temperature to medium-low, cover, and cook for 1 hour. Add the mushrooms and remove 2 cups of broth. Cover and continue cooking for 15 more minutes.
3. In a pan, pour the broth you reserved and the 2 teaspoons of fine cornmeal. Cook at medium-high temperature until the broth thickens. Stir constantly, to eliminate lumps. Rectify the seasoning to taste.

Japanese Style Skewers

Servings: 6

Calories: 190

Preparation time: 5 minute

Cook time: 6 minutes

Ingredients

- 1 pound of loin steak
- ½ cup scallions
- Wooden sticks for skewers

Marinated:

- 1 cup soy sauce
- 1 tbsp chopped garlic
- ½ cup rice vinegar
- 1 tbsp brown sugar

Peanut sauce:

- ¾ cup peanut butter
- ½ cup double cream
- ½ cup soy sauce
- 1 tbsp Asian style chili sauce
- ½ squeezed lemon

Steps to Cook

1. In a bowl, add the marinade and meat ingredients. Combine, cover and marinate for 15 minutes in the refrigerator.
2. Spread the meat on the wooden sticks to form the skewer. Leave free space on one side, to grab them more easily.
3. Add the peanut sauce ingredients, cover and blend at high speed for 30 seconds.
4. Preheat the pot at medium-high temperature for 3 minutes. Immediately reduce the temperature to medium, place the skewers and cook for 3 minutes per side, or until well cooked.
5. Meanwhile, in the 8-inch pan, heat the sauce over medium heat for 4 minutes.
6. Decorate the skewers with scallions and serve immediately with the peanut sauce.

Osso Buco

Servings: 6

Calories: 190

Preparation time: 5 minute

Cook time: 47 minutes

Ingredients	Steps to Cook

Ingredients

- 2 pounds (1 kg) beef bear
- 8 cups beef stock
- ½ pound (¼ kg) of carrot, cut into large squares
- ½ pound (¼ kg) of celery, cut into pieces
- 1 cup yellow onion, diced
- 2 teaspoons garlic, finely chopped
- 3 cups of tomato
- 1 cup red wine

Steps to Cook

1. Make cuts at the edges of the ossobuco so that it does not wrinkle. Season the fillets with salt and pepper and flour.
2. In the express pot, pour the extra virgin olive oil. Heat over high heat. Brown the osso buco fillets on both sides, remove and reserve.
3. Meanwhile, cut the leek and chives into small pieces.
4. In the same express pot, take advantage of the oil that was left when cooking the meat. Sauté the onion and leek for 90 seconds over high heat.
5. After time, add the crushed tomato, mix and cook for 60 seconds.
6. Add the red wine and let it evaporate for 2 minutes.
7. Next, add the osso buco fillets and add the meat stock.

Sausages To Beer

Servings: 6
Calories: 40
Preparation time: 5 minute
Cook time: 12 minutes

Ingredients

- 2 pounds sausage
- 2 14 oz cans of saurekraut, drained
- 1 cup brown sugar
- 12 oz of your favorite beer

For the filling and serve:

- 2 tbsp of oil
- 1 bell pepper, sliced
- 1 large onion, sliced
- ½ cup barbecue sauce
- ½ cup juices from the pot after cooking
- Hot dog bread

Steps to Cook

1. Cut the smoked sausage into long pieces. Place in the bottom of the clay pot. Top with drained sour kraut. Combine brown sugar and beer in bowl and pour over sausage and kraut. Put the pot on low heat and cook for 8 hours.
2. At some point during the 12 minutes, sauté your bell pepper and onion. After the sausages are done cooking, pour ½ cup of the juice from the pot and mix it with ½ cup of your favorite barbecue sauce. This will make a FANTASTIC dressing for your sausages! To serve, place the sausages and kraut on the buns, top with bell peppers and onions, if desired, and pour a little sauce on top. Eat fast, because it will be messy! Enjoy!

Lamb In Instant Pot

Ingredients

- 800 g leg of lamb
- 75 g flour
- frying oil
- 400 g mushrooms
- 2 onions
- 2 cloves garlic
- 2 tsp tomato puree
- 1 glass of sherry wine
- bay leaf and parsley
- cinnamon stick

Steps to Cook

1. Cut the meat into slices of 100 g each, season with salt and pepper. Coat in flour, fry until lightly browned. Add the finely chopped onions, when they turn color, add the bay leaf, cinnamon, some parsley in a sprig, and sherry; the tomato puree, 1 dl of water, the mushrooms (previously clean and sautéed in oil with the chopped garlic and parsley), season with salt and pepper.
2. Cover the pot and when the steam comes out of the valve, put on medium pressure and leave for 12 to 15 minutes over medium heat.
3. Cool the pot, open and serve the lamb slices on a tabletop, surrounded by the mushrooms and sauce. Exquisite and easy.

Minced Pork

Servings: 6

Calories: 370

Preparation time: 5 minute

Cook time: 45 minutes

Ingredients

- 4 lbs boneless pork
- 1 can of root beer
- 2 garlic cloves, minced
- 1 cup barbecue sauce
- 3 tbsp of pork dough or use the dough recipe below

Pork dough:

- 1 tbsp of paprika
- 2 tbsp of brown sugar
- ¾ tsp garlic powder
- ¾ tsp onion powder
- 1 tsp dried mustard
- ½ teaspoon salt
- ½ tsp black pepper

Steps to Cook

1. Cut pork into large cubes, about 4 "each, and season with pork.
2. Turn Instant Pot on the sear and add 2 tablespoons of oil. Brown the pork in batches until golden brown (or in a pan).
3. Deglaze the pan with ½ cup of water making sure to scrape off all the brown parts. Add garlic and root beer.
4. Add pork and cook at high pressure for 45 minutes. Natural release for 15 minutes.
5. Remove the pork from the instant pot and with two forks, mince the meat. Add ¼ cup juices from instant pot (discard remaining juices). Add the BBQ sauce.
6. Serve on toasted rolls with coleslaw.

Beef Stew

Servings: 4

Calories: 347

Preparation time: 5 minute

Cook time: 15 minutes

Ingredients

- 1 pound fat-free beef, diced
- 1 inch
- 1 cup of water
- 1 large onion sliced
- 4 small potatoes in quarters
- 1 cup frozen green beans
- 1 cup sliced carrots
- 1 cup diced tomatoes
- 1 teaspoon salt
- ¼ cup cold water
- 1 tablespoon flour

Steps to Cook

1. Put the beef, water and onion in the pot. Close and secure the lid. Place the pressure regulator on the vent tube and cook 8 minutes once the pressure regulator begins to rock slowly. Cool the pot quickly.
2. Add potatoes, green beans, carrots, tomatoes, salt and pepper in the pot. Close and secure the lid. Place the pressure regulator on the vent tube and cook 3 minutes once the pressure regulator begins to rock slowly. Cool the pot quickly.
3. Mix the water and flour. Stir and add to the stew. Heat until the stew thickens, stirring constantly.

Chapter 4

Fish and Seafood

Garlic Butter Shrimp And Rice

Servings: 1
Calories: 220
Preparation time: 5 minutes
Cook time: 10 minutes

Ingredients

- ½ to ¾ pounds Shrimp, peeled and deveined.
- 1 glass Basmati rice, well rinsed and drained
- 1 glass chicken broth
- ¾ teaspoon Salt or according to your taste
- ¼ tsp black pepper
- 2 to 4 pinches Red pepper flakes

Steps to Cook

1. Press Instant Pot to skip the mode. When hot, add 4 tablespoons of butter and chopped garlic. Cook, stirring occasionally for about 1 to 2 minutes. Make sure the garlic to turn pale golden (no darker).
2. Press cancel, add all the ingredients in group 1 and stir well. Remove the instant pot, close the lid and adjust the valve to seal. Select the rice mode. When the cooking time is over, let the instant pot be in warm mode for 4 minutes. When you have finished 4 minutes, turn the valve to vent and let the pressure release. Press "cancel" and open the lid. Gently add the remaining tablespoon of butter, grated Parmesan cheese and parsley.

Paella shrimp

Servings: 6

Calories: 220

Preparation time: 5 minutes

Cook time: 10 minutes

Ingredients

- 2 cups white onion
- 1 tbsp vegetable oil
- ½ cup of rice
- ¾ cup chicken broth
- 1 cup red bell pepper
- ½ bottle of saffron
- ¼ tbsp of paprika
- 24 g of chorizo
- ½ cup of stuffed olive
- 500 g of shrimp

Steps to Cook

1. Set Instant Pot to Saute function. Add butter to the pot and melt. Add onions and cook until smooth. Add garlic and cook for about one more minute. Add paprika, turmeric, salt, black pepper, red pepper flakes, and saffron threads. Stir and cook for about 1 minute.
2. Add the red peppers. Add rice and stir. Cook for about 30 seconds to 1 minute. Add the chicken stock and white wine.
3. Deglaze the pot by stirring to make sure there are no foods stuck to the bottom of the pot. Add shrimp on top. Turn off the instant pot and cover.
4. Make sure the valve is configured to seal. Set Instant Pot to manual mode and set a 5 minute timer. When done, quick release. Remove shrimp from pot and peel if desired. Serve with coriander.

Tuna Curry With Quinoa

Servings: 4
Calories: 344
Preparation time: 5 minutes
Cook time: 15 minutes

Ingredients

- 1½ pounds tuna
- Curry powder to taste
- Juice of 1 green lemon
- ¼ cup onion, diced
- ½ cup leek
- 2 cups quinoa, uncooked
- 2 cups of water
- 1 cup coconut milk
- ½ cup white wine (optional)
- Salt and black pepper to taste

Steps to Cook

1. In a bowl, season the tuna with curry powder, salt, black pepper and lemon juice; mix well. Cover and marinate for 5 minutes in the refrigerator.
2. Preheat the pot at medium-high temperature or until, after spraying a few drops of water, they roll on the surface without evaporating. Add onion and leek, and cook for 2 minutes; stir constantly.
3. Add the marinated tuna and cook for 2 more minutes, uncovered. Add quinoa, water, coconut milk and wine.
4. Cover with the valve open and cook at the same temperature until it whistles (in approximately 2 minutes). Reduce the temperature to low and, when the valve stops whistling, close it and cook for 8 minutes.

Pasta With Shrimp And Vegetables In Coconut Milk

Servings: 4-6

Calories: 757.5

Preparation time: 10 minutes

Cook time: 36 minutes

Ingredients

- 12 pounds pasta
- 1 cup mushroom cream
- 1 cup coconut milk
- 1 green pepper
- 1 red pepper
- 1 yellow pepper
- ¼ white onion
- 1 cup cherry tomatoes
- 1 sprig of cilantro
- 1 sliced celery stalk
- 2 pounds (1 kg) shrimp
- Parmesan cheese to taste
- Salt and black pepper to taste

Steps to Cook

1. Fill pot with water, cover with the valve open and cook at medium-high temperature until it whistles (in about 7 minutes). Add the pasta and cook for 8 minutes without covering, or until al dente. Drain with the Small Strainer. In a skillet, add the mushroom cream and coconut milk. Cook at medium temperature for 7 minutes; stir constantly.
2. Preheat a pan at medium-high temperature for 3 minutes. Add all the vegetables. Cook at medium-high temperature for 3 minutes, while stirring constantly. Add the shrimp and cook for 2 more minutes.
3. Add the prepared sauce and cooked pasta; stir well. Cover with the valve open until it whistles (approximately 2 to 3 minutes). Reduce the temperature to low, close the Valve and cook for 7 more minutes. Sprinkle Parmesan cheese over pasta and serve.

Salmon Mustard Steak

Servings: 4-6

Calories: 218

Preparation time: 10 minutes

Cook time: 36 minutes

Ingredients	Steps to Cook

Ingredients

- 4 salmon steaks 1 inch thick
- 4 tbsp of mustard
- 3 to 4 sprigs of fresh thyme or ½ teaspoon of dried thyme
- 1 tablespoon olive or vegetable oil
- 1 small onion, chopped
- 1 clove of minced garlic
- 1 cup dry white wine or chicken broth
- 1 bay leaf
- 2 tbsp mustard
- 1 tablespoon cornstarch

Steps to Cook

1. Spread each steak with 1 tablespoon of mustard. Crush 1 sprig of thyme in the mustard on each steak or sprinkle with dried thyme.
2. Pour oil into the pot. Saute onions and garlic over medium heat until tender. Add the wine and bay leaf and stir. Put the steaks on the rack of the pot. Close and secure the lid.
3. Place the pressure regulator on the vent tube and cook 2 minutes once the pressure regulator begins to rock slowly.
4. Cool the pot quickly. Carefully remove steaks and rack. Keep the steaks warm. Throw the bay leaf. Mix 2 tablespoons of mustard with the cornstarch.
5. Add to the Instant Pot liquid and stir. Heat until the sauce boils and thickens, stirring constantly.
6. Serve the sauce with the salmon steaks.

Tilapia Bruschetta Style

Servings: 12
Calories: 192
Preparation time: 5 minutes
Cook time: 18 minutes

Ingredients

- 6 pounds (3 kg) of tilapia fillets
- 2 pounds (1 kg) of cherry tomatoes, chopped in half
- 1 pound (½ kg) fresh mozzarella cheese, chopped into small pieces
- 1 cup chopped basil in thin strips
- 1 orange cut in half
- ½ cup balsamic vinegar
- Grated Parmesan cheese, to taste
- Seasoning for fish to taste

Steps to Cook

1. Season tilapia with seasoning for fish to taste.
2. Preheat the pot at medium-high temperature for about 3 minutes or until, after spraying a few drops of water, they roll over the surface without evaporating.
3. Immediately add half of the tilapia fillets and cover with half of the ingredients (except Parmesan cheese). Repeat.
4. Cover with the valve open and cook at the same temperature, until the valve whistles (in about 10 minutes). Reduce the temperature to medium-low and, when the valve stops whistling, close it and continue cooking for an additional 8 minutes.
5. When the tilapias are cooked, sprinkle Parmesan cheese to taste.
6. Serve immediately with white rice.

Shrimp Cau

Servings: 4

Calories: 188

Preparation time: 5 minutes

Cook time: 12 minutes

Ingredients

- 2 pounds (1 kg) of peeled medium shrimp
- ¼ cup diced onion
- 1 teaspoon finely chopped garlic
- 1 teaspoon cumin
- 1 teaspoon ground turmeric
- 1 sachet of achiote and coriander powder
- 2 cups diced potatoes
- 1 cup diced carrots
- 1 cup peas
- ¼ cup chopped mint
- 2 cups chicken broth
- Salt and black pepper to taste

Steps to Cook

1. Season tilapia with seasoning for fish to taste.
2. Preheat the pot at medium-high temperature for 3 minutes. Add the onion, garlic and shrimp; Skip for 1 minute while stirring constantly.
3. Add the cumin, turmeric and achiote. Keep stirring for 30 seconds.
4. Add potatoes, carrots and other ingredients. Cover with the valve open and cook until it whistles (in about 2 minutes). Reduce the temperature to medium and close the valve. Cook for about 8 more minutes, or until the potato is soft.
5. Serve with your favorite rice.

Salmon with creamy herb and parmesan sauce

Servings: 4

Calories: 655.7

Preparation time: 5 minutes

Cook time: 11 minutes

Ingredients

- 4 frozen salmon fillets
- ½ cup of water
- 1.5 teaspoons minced garlic
- ½ cup thick cream
- 1 cup grated Parmesan cheese
- 1 tablespoon chopped fresh chives
- 1 tablespoon chopped fresh parsley
- 1 tbsp of fresh dill
- 1 teaspoon of fresh lemon juice
- Salt and pepper to taste

Steps to Cook

1. Put water and garlic in the insert with the trivet on top. Place the salmon on the trivet.
2. Close the pressure cooker and set it to Manual for 4-5 minutes. *
3. Once the timer goes off, quickly release the pressure. Remove the salmon and trivet from the pot.
4. Turn off the pressure cooker and set it to Skip and set it to Normal.
5. Once the water begins to boil, beat the heavy cream and bring to a boil again. Boil for about 2-3 minutes. The mixture should be able to stick to the back of a spoon.
6. Turn off pressure cooker and remove insert from heat. Whisk the chives, parsley, dill, Parmesan cheese, and lemon juice. Salt and pepper to taste.

Fish Soup

Servings: 8

Calories: 72

Preparation time: 5 minutes

Cook time: 12 minutes

Ingredients

- 4 pounds chicken
- Salt and black pepper to taste
- 6 cups chickpeas
- 1 cup carrots, sliced
- ½ cup onion, diced
- ¼ cup cilantro chopped
- 2 cloves garlic chopped
- 3 chipotle peppers
- 10 cups of water

Garrison:

- 1 avocado, sliced
- 4 radishes, sliced
- Tortillas in strips
- Lemon slices

Steps to Cook

1. In the pressure cooker, add the chicken, previously seasoned with salt and black pepper, and the rest of the ingredients. Do not fill the unit more than two thirds of its capacity.

2. Cover, close and cook at medium-high temperature. Once the throttle valve whistles and releases steam, reduce the temperature to medium and cook for 30 minutes. Make sure the regulator has released steam before continuing cooking.

3. Turn off the burner, turn the regulator valve indicator to the pressure release icon, and allow all steam to be released before opening the lid. The correct way to know is when the red indicator goes down. Make sure the chickpeas are well cooked. If necessary, add salt and black pepper to taste. Serve with avocado, radishes, strip tortillas and lemon slices.

Broccoli And Cod With Lemon And Dill

Servings: 4

Calories: 103

Preparation time: 3 minutes

Cook time: 2 minutes

Ingredients

- 1 pound frozen cod fillets 1 inch thick
- Dried dill
- Pepper with lemon
- Salt
- 1 cup of water
- 2 cups broccoli in snacks

Steps to Cook

1. Cut the fish into 4 pieces. Sprinkle with dried dill, pepper with lemon and salt. Pour the water into the pot. Accommodate the fish and the Broccoli on the rack of the pot.
2. Close and secure the lid. Place the pressure regulator on the vent tube and cook 2 minutes once the pressure regulator begins to rock slowly. Cool the pot quickly.

Chapter 5

Salads, Soups and Sauces

Servings: 4

Calories: 364

Preparation time: 1 minute

Cook time: 35-40 minutes

Chickpeas

Ingredients	Steps to Cook

Ingredients

- 1 pound dried chickpeas
- 6-8 cups of water
- 1 teaspoon salt optional

Steps to Cook

1. Add the chickpeas, salt and enough water to cover the chickpeas 1 ½ - 2 inches in a 6-quart instant pot.
2. Set Instant Pot to high pressure and cook for 30-35 minutes al dente.
3. Allow a 10 minute natural pressure release.

Minestrone Soup

Servings: 4

Calories: 110

Preparation time: 5 minutes

Cook time: 20 minutes

Ingredients

- 1 pound of fat-free beef
- 5 cups of water
- 1 can diced tomatoes
- ½ cup chopped onion
- 1 cup sliced carrots
- ¼ cup chopped celery
- 1 clove of minced garlic
- 2 tbsp dried parsley
- 1 ½ teaspoons basil
- 1 teaspoon salt
- 1 bay leaf
- ¼ tsp black pepper
- 1 can white beans
- 1 can green beans
- 2 ounces fine noodles

Steps to Cook

1. Put beef, water, tomatoes, onions, carrots, celery, parsley, basil, salt, bay leaf and pepper inside the pot.
2. Close and secure the lid. Place the pressure regulator on the vent tube and cook 10 minutes once the pressure regulator begins to rock slowly.
3. Let the pressure decrease on its own. Add medium white beans, green beans and noodles.
4. Simmer without lid for 10 minutes. Garnish with Parmesan cheese if desired.

Tarasca Soup

Servings: 4

Calories: 114

Preparation time: 5 minutes

Cook time: 9 minutes

Ingredients

- 2 cups black beans
- 1 cup pinto beans
- 1 cup tomato sauce
- ¼ cup tomatoes
- 1 pound of chipotle chili
- 1 tbsp chopped garlic
- 6 cups chicken broth
- 1 cup double cream
- Lemon green to taste
- 1 sliced avocado
- Sour cream to taste
- 1 cup tortilla strips
- Salt and black pepper

Steps to Cook

1. Blend the beans, tomato sauce, dried tomatoes, chipotle chili sauce, garlic and 1 cup of chicken broth, until you get a thick puree.
2. In the pot, add the remaining cups of chicken broth and the blended mixture; stir well. Close the valve and cook at medium-high temperature until it whistles (in about 5 minutes).
3. Add the double cream and stir. Reduce the temperature to low. If necessary, add salt and pepper to taste. Cover with the valve closed and cook for 4 more minutes.
4. Serve with sour cream to taste, avocado and green lemon. Spread the tortillas in strips over the soup.

Mediterranean Bean Salad

Servings: 4

Calories: 175

Preparation time: 5 min.

Cook time: 30 minutes

Ingredients

- 15.5 ounces chick peas
- 15 ounces black beans
- 1 cup tomatoes
- 1 large garlic clove
- ½ cup red onion
- ¼ cup fresh parsley
- ¼ cup fresh mint
- 1 ½ tbsp of olive oil
- Juice of 1 medium lemon
- ½ teaspoon kosher salt
- Freshly ground black pepper

Steps to Cook

1. In a large bowl, combine the beans, tomatoes, garlic, onion, parsley, and mint.
2. For the dressing, in a small bowl, beat the olive oil and lemon juice until smooth and emulsified.
3. Pour the dressing over the beans and vegetables, add ½ teaspoon of salt and black pepper to taste and mix carefully with a large metal spoon. Let stand at room temperature for 30 minutes so that the flavors combine.

Lasagna Soup

Servings: 4
Calories: 441
Preparation time: 5 min
Cook time: 30 minutes

Ingredients

- 1 pound of soft Italian sausage
- 1 medium onion
- 2 tsp minced garlic
- ½ teaspoon salt
- ¼ tsp black pepper
- 3 cups chicken broth
- 14 oz tomatoes
- 1/3 cup frozen spinach
- 8 lasagna noodles in small pieces
- grated mozzarella
- Parmesan cheese
- fresh parsley to serve

Steps to Cook

1. In a medium skillet, cook the Italian sausage and onion over medium-high heat until the sausage is browned, stirring frequently.
2. Add garlic, Italian seasoning, salt and pepper. Pour into the Instant Pot.
3. Add the broth, tomatoes, pasta sauce and spinach. Cover and simmer for 6 hours or high for 3 hours.
4. Open the lid, add the broken lasagna noodles and cook for 30 minutes or until tender. Serve with cheese and fresh parsley as desired.

Coconut Milk Chicken Soup

Servings: 6
Calories: 141.5
Preparation time: 5 min
Cook time: 20 minutes

Ingredients

- ½ kg chicken breast
- ½ cup chopped scallion
- 1 cup red peppers
- 1 tsp chopped garlic
- 1 tsp chopped ginger
- 1 cup mushrooms
- 1 tsp grated lemon peel
- 1 tsp chopped cilantro
- 1 tsp chopped basil
- 8 cups of water
- 1 cup coconut milk
- Sea salt and black pepper to taste
- Lemon green to taste

Steps to Cook

1. Preheat the pot at medium-high temperature for about 3 minutes, or until a few drops of water are sprayed, they bounce off the surface without evaporating. Cook the chicken cubes for 4 minutes, while stirring constantly with the spatula.
2. Add the rest of the ingredients (except water and coconut milk). Cook for 2 more minutes, while stirring.
3. Pour the water and coconut milk. Close the valve and cook until it whistles, in about 6 minutes.
4. Reduce the temperature to low, adjust the seasoning to taste and let cook for 7 more minutes with the lid on and the valve closed. Serve immediately with a few drops of lemon.

Chapter 6

Vegetarian and Vegan | Sides and Mains

Artichokes In Sauce

Servings: 4

Calories: 60

Preparation time: 5 min

Cook time: 10 minutes

Ingredients	Steps to Cook

Ingredients

- 1 cup of water
- 1 tablespoon vegetable oil
- 3 artichokes

Steps to Cook

1. Pour water and oil into the pot. Put the artichokes on the pot rack. Close and secure the lid. Place the pressure regulator on the vent tube and cook 10 minutes once the pressure regulator begins to rock slowly.
2. Cool the pot quickly. Serve with garlic sauce.
3. **Garlic Sauce:** Combine ¼ cup of melted butter and 2 cloves of minced garlic. Serve hot.

Low cost & high taste...

Asian Salad

Servings: 2

Calories: 224

Preparation time: 5 min

Cook time: 10 minutes

Ingredients

- ¼ cup lemon juice
- 2 tsp soy sauce
- 1 jalapeño, chopped
- 2 tsp of vegetable oil
- ½ tsp of sugar
- 4 cups red cabbage
- 1 cup grated carrots
- 1 cup coriander leaves
- 1 cup fresh mint leaves

Steps to Cook

Royal Prestige Dressing:

1. In the mixing bowl, add the onion, salt, black pepper and lemon juice; mix well. Incorporate cilantro, honey and olive oil. Stir and reserve in the refrigerator.

Salad:

2. In the pot add the balsamic vinegar and cook at medium-high temperature for 4 minutes or until it boils. Reduce the temperature to medium and continue cooking for 5 minutes.

Low cost & high taste...

Servings: 6

Calories: 244.2

Preparation time: 18 minutes

Quinoa Tabbouleh

Ingredients

- 3 cups quinoa
- 6 cups of water or chicken broth
- 1½ cups tomatoes
- 1½ cups cucumber
- ½ cup purple onion
- ¼ cup chopped parsley
- ¾ cup chopped mint
- ¾ cup red pepper
- ¾ cup green pepper
- 1 tablespoon olive oil
- Juice of 1 green lemon
- Salt and black pepper to taste

Steps to Cook

1. Rinse quinoa in a fine mesh strainer. In the 4-quart pot, add quinoa and water. Cover with the valve open and cook at medium-high temperature until it whistles (approximately 5 minutes).
2. Reduce the temperature to low and, when the valve stops whistling, close it and cook for 13 minutes.
3. Carefully remove the quinoa from the pot and let it cool in the refrigerator for about 20 minutes.
4. Combine all ingredients well in the 5-quart Mixing Bowl and serve.

Salad With Balsamic Dressing

Servings: 2

Calories: 170

Preparation time: 10 minutes

Ingredients

- 1 diced carrot
- 1 diced zucchini
- 1cup lettuce
- ½ cup cherry tomatoes, chopped in half
- ½ cup balsamic vinegar
- Salt and black pepper to taste

Steps to Cook

1. In the pot, add 2 ounces of water and chopped vegetables. Cover and cook at medium-high temperature with the valve open, until it whistles (in about 3 minutes). Reduce the temperature to low and, when the valve stops whistling, close it and cook for 2 more minutes, or until the vegetables are al dente. Drain with the Small Strainer.

2. Meanwhile, pour the balsamic vinegar into the 1-quarter kettle. Cook at medium temperature for about 7 minutes, or until the vinegar is reduced by approximately half. Serve right away, and sprinkle the balsamic vinegar.

Low cost & high taste...

Servings: 8

Calories: 77

Preparation time: 5 minutes

Cooking time: 3 minutes

Edible Roots Glazed

Ingredients

- 2 butter spoons
- 2 medium turnips
- 8 ounces small carrots
- 2 medium peeled parsnips, sliced ½ inch thick
- 1 cup chicken broth
- 2 tsp sugar
- 2 tsp ground ginger
- ¼ cup cold water
- 1 tbsp cornstarch
- Salt and pepper to taste

Steps to Cook

1. Heat the butter in the pressure cooker over medium heat.
2. Add the turnips and carrots and sauté 3 minutes. Add parsnips, chicken broth, ginger and sugar. Close and secure the lid. Place the pressure regulator on the vent tube and cook
3. 1 minute once the pressure regulator starts to rock slowly. Cool the pot quickly. Mix the water with the cornstarch. Add the sauce and stir. Heat until the sauce thickens, stirring constantly.

Grilled asparagus

Servings: 4

Calories: 45

Preparation time: 5 minutes

Cooking time: 5 minutes

Ingredients

- ½ pound (¼ kg) of fresh asparagus
- 1 tablespoon olive oil
- Salt and black pepper to taste

Steps to Cook

1. In the bowl, mix the olive oil with salt and pepper to taste. Add the asparagus and cover them well.
2. Preheat the pot at medium-high temperature for 3 minutes. Add the asparagus and cook for 2 minutes per side. Serve right away.

Glazed Sweet Potatoes With Maple Syrup

Servings: 6

Calories: 161.1

Preparation time: 5 minutes

Cooking time: 5 minutes

Ingredients

- 3 peeled sweet potatoes in pieces between 1 and 1½ inches
- ¾ cup maple syrup
- ½ cup of water
- 1 tablespoon melted butter
- ½ teaspoon salt

Steps to Cook

1. Put the sweet potatoes in the pressure cooker. Combine the remaining ingredients and pour them over the sweet potatoes.

2. Close and secure the lid. Place the pressure regulator on the vent tube and cook 5 minutes once the pressure regulator begins to rock slowly. Cool the pot quickly.

Mashed Potatoes With Garlic

Servings: 6

Calories: 252

Preparation time: 5 minutes

Cooking time: 5 minutes

Ingredients

- 2 pounds of reddish potatoes, peeled, diced
- 4 large garlic cloves
- 1½ cups chicken broth
- 1 tablespoon butter
- Salt and pepper to taste

Steps to Cook

1. Put all ingredients, except butter, salt and pepper, in the pot. Close and secure the lid. Place the pressure regulator on the vent tube and cook 5 minutes once the pressure regulator begins to rock slowly.

2. Cool the pot quickly. Let the potatoes, garlic and broth rest in the pot.

3. Mash the potatoes with a hand stomp until you reach the desired consistency. Add the butter. Season with salt and pepper.

Cabbage With Apples

Servings: 6

Calories: 94.7

Preparation time: 2 minutes

Cooking time: 4 minutes

Ingredients

- 8 cups cabbage in strips
- 1 small onion, finely sliced
- 1 small apple for pie, peeled, without the center and cut
- ½ cup chicken broth
- 2 tablespoons frozen apple juice, thawed
- Salt and pepper to taste

Steps to Cook

1. Add all the ingredients to the pot. Close and secure the lid. Place the pressure regulator on the vent tube and cook 4 minutes once the pressure regulator begins to sway slowly. Cool the pot quickly.

Lentil Curry

Servings: 6

Calories: 126

Preparation time: 2 minutes

Cooking time: 3 minutes

Ingredients

- 1 tablespoon vegetable oil
- ¾ cup chopped onion
- 3 cups of water
- 1 cup lentils
- ½ tablespoon coriander
- ½ tablespoon curry powder
- ½ teaspoon ground ginger
- ½ teaspoon salt

Steps to Cook

1. Pour oil into the pot. Sauté the onions over medium heat. Add water, lentils, cilantro, curry powder and ginger. Closing and secure the lid. Place the pressure regulator on the vent tube and cook 3 minutes once the pressure regulator begins to rock slowly. Let the pressure decrease on its own. Add salt and stir.

1-Minute Quinoa in Instant Pot

Servings: 6

Calories: 126

Preparation time: 2 minutes

Cooking time: 3 minutes

Ingredients	Steps to Cook

Ingredients

- 1 cup dried quinoa
- 2 cups of water

Steps to Cook

1. Place the quinoa and water in the stainless steel insert of your instant pot. Close the lid and adjust the valve to the "sealed" position. Press "manual" and set the timer to 1 minute.

2. The pressure cooker will beep shortly and start pressing. It only takes a few minutes. Once this is done, Instant Pot will beep again. Press the "cancel/turn off" button. Do not release pressure.

3. Let the pressure cooker release the pressure naturally for about 3 to 4 minutes. Then change the valve to the "vent" position and relieve the pressure.

4. Carefully open the lid away from your face. The liquid must be completely absorbed by the quinoa. Stir in the quinoa. It should be fluffy.

Chapter 4

Mediterranean Deserts and Snacks

Vanilla Pastry Cream

Servings: 4

Calories: 137

Preparation time: 5 minutes

Cook time: 5 minutes

Ingredients	Steps to Cook

Ingredients

- 2 cups low fat milk
- 2 lightly beaten eggs
- ¼ cup sugar
- ¼ teaspoon salt
- ½ teaspoon of vanilla
- Nutmeg
- 1 cup of water

Steps to Cook

1. Combine milk, eggs, sugar, salt and vanilla and pour into individual cups for custard. Sprinkle with nutmeg.
2. Cover each cup firmly with the foil. Pour the water into the pot. Position the cups on the rack of the pot.
3. Close and secure the lid. Place the pressure regulator on the vent tube and cook 5 minutes once the pressure regulator begins to rock slowly.
4. Cool the pot quickly. Let the cream cool well in the refrigerator.

Small Pumpkin Pastry Cream

Servings: 8
Calories: 207
Preparation time: 5 minutes
Cook time: 10 minutes

Ingredients

- 1 can of 16 ounces of prepared pumpkin
- 1 14-ounce can sweetened condensed milk
- 3 beaten eggs
- 1 teaspoon finely chopped polished ginger (optional)
- 1 teaspoon ground cinnamon
- ¼ teaspoon ground cloves
- 1 cup of water

Steps to Cook

1. Mix the pumpkin, milk, eggs, cinnamon, ginger and cloves. Pour into individual cups for custard.
2. Cover each cup firmly with the foil. Pour the water into the pot. Position the cups on the rack of the pot. Close and secure the lid.
3. Place the pressure regulator on the vent tube and cook 10 minutes once the pressure regulator begins to rock slowly. Cool the pot quickly. Let the cream cool well in the refrigerator. If desired, serve with whipped cream.

Rice Pudding

Servings: 6

Calories: 238

Preparation time: 5 minutes

Cook time: 13 minutes

Ingredients

- 1 cup large grain white rice
- 1½ cups of water
- 1 cup of water
- 1 cup whole milk
- ½ cup sugar
- ½ cup raisins
- ½ teaspoon cinnamon

Steps to Cook

1. Mix the rice and 1½ cups of water in a metal bowl that fits comfortably in the pot. Cover the bowl firmly with the foil. Pour 1 cup of water into the pot. Position the bowl on the rack of the pot.

2. Close and secure the lid. Place the pressure regulator on the vent tube and cook 10 minutes once the pressure regulator begins to rock slowly.

3. Cool the pot quickly. Add the milk, sugar, raisins and cinnamon to the rice, and stir. Cover the bowl firmly with the foil.

4. Position the bowl on the rack of the pot. Close and secure the lid. Place the pressure regulator on the vent tube and cook 3 minutes once the pressure regulator begins to rock slowly. Let the pressure decrease on its own.

Tapioca Pudding

Servings: 6

Calories: 113

Preparation time: 5 minutes

Cook time: 20 minutes

Ingredients

- 2 cups low fat milk
- 2 tablespoons quick-cooking tapioca
- 2 lightly beaten eggs
- ⅓ cup of sugar
- ½ teaspoon of vanilla
- 1 cup of water

Steps to Cook

1. Heat the milk and tapioca. Remove from heat and let stand 15 minutes.

2. Combine eggs, sugar and vanilla. Add milk and tapioca, stirring constantly.

3. Pour them into individual cups for custard. Cover each cup firmly with the foil. Pour the water into the pot.

4. Position the cups on the rack of the pot. Close and secure the lid.

5. Place the pressure regulator on the vent tube and cook 5 minutes once the pressure regulator begins to rock slowly.

6. Cool the pot quickly. Let the pudding cool well in the refrigerator.

Stuffed Apples

Servings: 4

Calories: 224

Preparation time: 5 minutes

Cook time: 40 minutes

Ingredients

- ¼ cup golden raisins
- ½ cup dry red wine
- ¼ cup chopped nuts
- 2 tablespoons sugar
- ½ teaspoon grated orange peel
- ½ teaspoon ground cinnamon
- 4 apples for cooking
- 1 tablespoon butter
- 1 cup of water

Steps to Cook

1. Soak the raisins in wine for approximately 30 minutes. Drain Keep the wine. Combine raisins, nuts, sugar, orange zest and cinnamon. Cut the center to the apples to the bottom but without piercing it. Peel the upper third of the apples.

2. Position each apple on a square of aluminum foil that is large enough to wrap the whole apple.

3. Fill the centers with the preparation of the raisins. Decorate the top of each apple with a quarter of the butter. Wrap apples with aluminum foil, squeezing the top tightly. Put the wine you kept, the water and the apples in the pot.

4. Place the pressure regulator on the vent tube and cook 10 minutes once the pressure regulator begins to rock slowly. Cool the pot quickly.

Apple Crisp With Oatmeal

Servings: 4

Calories: 209

Preparation time: 5 minutes

Cook time: 20 minutes

Ingredients

- 4 cups peeled apples and slices
- 1 tablespoon lemon juice
- ½ cup quick-cooking oatmeal
- ¼ cup brown sugar
- 2 tablespoons flour
- 1 teaspoon cinnamon
- 2 tablespoons soft butter
- 2 cups of water

Steps to Cook

1. Spray apples with lemon juice. Combine oatmeal, brown sugar, flour and cinnamon.
2. Cut and add the butter to the oatmeal mixture until a lumpy dough forms. Place the apples in an oiled bowl that fits comfortably in the pot. Spray the oatmeal mixture evenly over apples. Cover the bowl firmly with the foil.
3. Pour the water into the pot. Position the bowl on the rack of the pot. Close and secure the lid.
4. Place the pressure regulator on the vent tube and cook 20 minutes once the pressure regulator begins to slowly swing. Cool the pot quickly.

Cheesecake

Servings: 6
Calories: 305
Preparation time: 5 minutes
Cook time: 15 minutes

Ingredients

- 1 package of 8 ounces cream cheese
- 1 package of 3 ounces of cream cheese
- ½ cup sugar
- 2 eggs
- ½ cup vanilla wafer crumbs
- 2½ cups of water

Steps to Cook

1. Beat the cream cheese until uniform. Add sugar and eggs, and beat. Pour into cups for pastry cream. Spray with vanilla wafer crumbs. Cover each cup firmly with the foil. Pour the water into the pot.

2. Position the cups on the rack of the pot. Close and secure the lid.

3. Place the pressure regulator on the vent tube and cook 15 minutes once the pressure regulator begins to rock slowly.

4. Cool the pot quickly. Chill the cheesecake.

5. Pass a thin knife through the inner wall of the cups and invest in serving plates.

6. Let cool well in the refrigerator. If desired, cover with one of the following sauces.

Carrot Cake

Servings: 8
Calories: 360
Preparation time: 5 minutes
Cook time: 45 minutes

Ingredients

- 1 cup of flour
- 1 teaspoon baking powder
- 1 teaspoon of baking soda
- 1 teaspoon cinnamon
- 2 eggs
- ¾ cup brown sugar
- ½ cup of oil
- 2 cups grated carrot
- ½ cup chopped walnuts

Steps to Cook

1. Put the eggs into a deep bowl, and then add the sugar. Mix well with an electric mixer. Add the oil until it is incorporated. Two tablespoons of flour are reserved and the rest is hovered with baking powder, baking soda, cinnamon and a pinch of salt.

2. Then the mixture obtained. At the beginning add to the flour in an enveloping form without overshoot. Then add the grated carrot and mix well. Separately the two tablespoons of flour are combined with raisins and nuts. This, to prevent them from going to the bottom of the pot when they are added to the dough.

3. The mixture is then poured into the Instant Pot, covered and the valve removed. Put on low heat and left until it is cooked, on average it is 45 minutes on low heat so that the cake is ready.

Pumpkin Flan

Servings: 4
Calories: 175.6
Preparation time: 15 minutes
Cook time: 30 minutes

Ingredients

- 400 g pumpkin pulp
- 370 g condensed milk
- 4 eggs
- 1 teaspoon sugary vanilla

For the candy:

- 3 tablespoons sugar
- 1 tablespoon water
- 1 tablespoon lemon juice

Steps to Cook

1. Roast the pumpkin. Put two pieces of pumpkin with skin in a baking dish, put at 200°C. Until it is tender, remove the pulp and go through the parade, let cool.

2. Put the sugar, the water and the lemon juice in, bring it to the fire. When it is caramelized, tilt and turning it to caramelize the sides. Remove from heat.

3. Put the pot on the fire, uncovered, with water that covers half the flan. Let it warm up.

4. In a bowl, beat the eggs with the vanilla sugar, using the rods, add the pumpkin, stir, add the condensed milk. Mix well. Pour everything in the flan.

5. Cover and put in the pot. Cover the pot and let it cook for 30 minutes since the valve starts to spin. Turn off the heat, let cool to unmold.

Flan 3 Milks In A Water Bath In Instant Pot

Servings: 4

Calories: 175.6

Preparation time: 15 minutes

Cook time: 4 minutes

Ingredients

- 1 can condensed milk
- 1 can evaporated milk
- 3 eggs
- ½ can sugar
- 1 tablespoon vanilla
- 1 can semi milk

For the candy:

- 1 can sugar

Steps to Cook

1. For the caramel: in a pan put the sugar can with the water mix and put on medium heat, stir. Once it starts to boil (bubbles) stop moving because the sugar can crystallize, and leave it until it has amber color, (usually it takes about 4 min) then you will remove from the heat. Pour it into the mold, trying to cover both the bottom and the walls of this

2. While the caramel is cooking you can make the flan mixture. In a bowl pour the ingredients (evaporated milk, condensed, and semi) the 3 eggs, sugar and vanilla. With the manual mixer mix all the ingredients and pour them into the previously prepared mold.

3. Cover the mold with foil. And place it inside the express pot in Maria's bathroom. It is important that it is tightly closed so that water does not strain.

4. Count about 25 min since the pot takes pressure, turn off and let cool.

Cake With Berries

Ingredients

- 3 eggs
- A piece of butter
- 250 g of fresh or frozen berries
- 3 ml of lemon juice
- 250 g of sugar
- 2 g edible soda

Steps to Cook

1. Shake the eggs with sugar in a separate bowl.

2. Sift the flour. Sodas extinguish lemon juice. Stir the flour with soda and, little by little pouring the mixture, knead the dough.

3. Fresh berries resolve, remove and wrinkle. Rinse thoroughly under a tap and dry with a disposable towel. Frozen berries do not need to be washed.

4. Brush a piece of butter in the shape of the appliance, pour the dough into it and sprinkle the berries on top. Leave on for about 5 minutes until the berries are slightly "drowned" in the dough.

5. Start the "baking" function for one hour, close the lid firmly and press the "start" button. Remove the finished cake with a steam basket and sprinkle with powdered sugar.

Berry Cake With Sour Cream

Servings: 6
Calories: 234.6
Preparation time: 10 minutes
Cook time: 60 minutes

Ingredients	Steps to Cook

Ingredients

- 100 g margarine
- 200 g sour cream
- 300g granulated sugar
- Salt
- 1 ½ cup flour
- Two eggs
- Baking powder

Steps to Cook

1. Remove the margarine from the refrigerator and let it soften. Add half the sugar and grind carefully.
2. Break the eggs, add baking powder and beat. Add the margarine with sugar to the beaten eggs and mix. Pour the flour into small portions and knead fairly elastic dough.
3. Lubricate the shape of the device with oil and put the dough in it. Distribute evenly across the bottom and make high bumpers.
4. Spread the raspberries on the top, close the lid and activate the "baking" function for 1 hour.
5. Put sour cream on a gauze, folded in several layers, fold the bag and hang over the container to get rid of excess liquid.

Berry Cake With Curd

Servings: 4

Calories: 100

Preparation time: 10 minutes

Cook time: 60 minutes

Ingredients

Mass:

- 10 baking powder
- half a packet of butter
- 250 g of sugar
- 100 g flour

Filling:

- 250 g currants
- 250 g of cottage cheese
- 2 eggs
- 75 g sugar

Steps to Cook

1. For the cake take soft cottage cheese. Sweet pastry lovers can increase the amount of sugar.
2. Remove the butter from the refrigerator to soften it.
3. In a large bowl, mix the sifted flour with sugar and baking powder. Put the sliced butter and grind the dough into small pieces with your hands.
4. Beat the eggs lightly; add the eggs and the soft cottage cheese. Continue beating until we get a homogeneous blender.
5. Grease the device container with oil and place a strip of baking paper. Distribute approximately two thirds of the dough and distribute it evenly along the bottom, pressing it against the walls.
6. Pour the curd filling over the dough and level it. Put two tablespoons of crumb of the remaining dough. Distribute the rest of the filling evenly. Put the berries on top and sprinkle with crumbs.

Berry Sand Cake

Servings: 8

Calories: 100

Preparation time: 10 minutes

Cook time: 40 minutes

Ingredients

- A bag of vanilla
- ½ kg fresh or frozen berries
- ½ kg flour
- 250 g powdered sugar
- Egg
- A package of margarine Yolk

Steps to Cook

1. The cake can be baked with any type of berries. The amount of sugar depends on the selected variety of berries. If you are cooking with frozen berries, you should defrost them and leave them in a strainer to remove excess water. Then mix the berries with the sugar.

2. Beat an egg in a bowl, add the vanillin and pour a glass of sugar. Beat everything until smooth. Introduce the soft margarine. Sifted flour is gradually added to the egg and butter mixture. Knead fairly dense dough. Wrap it in a wrapper and put it in the fridge for 30 minutes.

3. Approximately ¼ part to go out to decorate. Spread the rest of the dough in a thin layer. Put it in a greased multi-well bowl, forming bumpers. Top spread the filling of the berries.

4. Divide the rest of the dough into small pieces, roll them into thin flails and place them on top of a pattern. Cook for 40 minutes.

Berry Sand Cake

Servings: 8

Calories: 100

Preparation time: 10 minutes

Cook time: 30 minutes

Ingredients

- 3 eggs
- 4 g of baking cake
- 250 g of sugar
- 40 g semolina
- A glass of flour
- A quarter of a packet of butter
- 200 g of berries

Steps to Cook

1. Take a dish deep enough and beat the eggs in lush foam. Gradually add sugar and vanilla, continue beating with a mixer until the sugar dissolves completely.

2. Now, add some flour with baking powder to the beaten eggs and knead the dough until it has a smooth and smooth texture without lumps.

3. Brush the bowl of the device with oil and mix it in the semolina. Now, cover it with baking paper to make it easier to get the cake.

4. Pour the dough into the bowl, spread the berries on top and press down slightly with a spatula.

5. Switch the appliance to baking mode for 45 minutes. Cool the cake slightly and remove the bowls by pulling the ends of the paper. Transfer the cake to a bowl and cut it into portions. Serve with any drink.

Berry Puff Pastry Cake

Servings: 3

Calories: 100

Preparation time: 10 minutes

Cook time: 30 minutes

Ingredients

- 60g sugar
- ½ kg puff pastry
- 100 ml cream
- A cup glass any berries without stones
- 200g cottage cheese

Steps to Cook

1. Defrost the dough beforehand and spread it, without rolling, in the instant pot bowl. Distribute, pressing on the bottom and walls.

2. Remove the curd cheese through a fine sieve, add the cream and sugar. Rub thoroughly.

3. Put the curd filling in the base.

4. Wash the berries and dry them on a disposable towel. Distributed evenly over the curd filling. Sprinkle with sugar. The amount is adjusted based on the acid in the berries.

5. Close the lid tightly, activate the baking mode and prepare the cake for forty minutes. Cool the cake slightly in a bowl, then carefully remove it and cut it into pieces. Served with any drink.

Strawberry Jam

Servings: 8

Calories: 85

Preparation time: 10 minutes

Cook time: 45 minutes

Ingredients

- 3 pounds of fresh strawberries (clean and chopped)
- 2 cups granulated white sugar
- Juice of one large lemon
- 1 tablespoon grated lemon zest

Optional:

- 2 tablespoons cornstarch (or more if necessary)
- 4 tablespoons of water

Steps to Cook

1. Wash the strawberries in cold water, with the stem still on, do not remove them before washing, as they will absorb additional water. Let them drain in a strainer for a few minutes, check for moldy or soft berries and discard them. Cut them into quarters and add them to Instant Pot and also add the sugar. Mix the strawberries and sugar and let them steep for 30 minutes, the strawberries will release extra juice.

2. Add lemon juice and lemon zest, stir again. Close and lock the lid, seal the valve and pressure cook for 1 minute, followed by a 15 minute natural pressure release. After which, turn the valve over and release the remaining pressure. Open the lid carefully, stir to combine. You can use an immersion blender to get the desired jam texture.

3. Select stir fry mode, stir mixture and bring to a boil.

Cake With Raspberries And Cottage Cheese

Servings: 6

Calories: 195

Preparation time: 15 minutes

Cook time: 60 minutes

Ingredients

- A glass or one and a half Raspberries
- 2510g Flour
- 2 yolks plus 2 whole eggs
- 125g Fridge Butter
- ½ cup granulated sugar
- Cottage cheese 300g
- 4 large spoons sour cream
- Vanilla sugar

Steps to Cook

1. For the sweet dough, all the ingredients must be cold, and it is necessary to cook them quickly and touch them as little as possible with the hands so as not to heat them. Therefore, cut the butter and flour with a knife and crush with a spoon. Quickly mix 2 egg yolks with sugar and pour the mixture into the oil crumb. Stir vigorously, put in a bag and place in the refrigerator for at least 30 minutes.

2. Cottage cheese, mix a blender with the remaining sugar, vanilla sugar and sour cream. Mix in the same two whole eggs.

3. Remove the dough from the refrigerator, spread it slightly and place it in the bowl, spreading it with your hands and forming the cake with the sides. Trim Put cheesecake inside, and raspberry on top.

4. Bake in a slow cooker for about 1 hour.

Chocolate And Oat Flakes

Servings: 4

Calories: 369.1

Preparation time: 2 minutes

Cook time: 20 minutes

Ingredients

- 1 cup oatmeal
- 2 cups unsweetened almond milk
- 1 cup of water
- 2 tablespoons cocoa
- 2 tablespoons maple honey or honey
- 1 tablespoon oil
- ½ teaspoon of vanilla
- Optional to put on top after:0
- ½ cup raspberries
- ½ cup chocolate chips

Steps to Cook

1. Put oil in the bottom of the pressure cooker to prevent the oatmeal from sticking.
2. Put all the ingredients in the pressure cooker, mixing well, so that the cocoa is completely broken.
3. Cook for 4 minutes at high pressure and turn off to allow the pressure to drop naturally.
4. Mix well and put the oatmeal in bowls and sprinkle with raspberries and chocolate chips, if desired.

Chocolate Cake Bites

Servings: 8

Calories: 424

Preparation time: 30 minutes

Cook time: 13 minutes

Ingredients

- 4 oz prefabricated cookie dough
- 6 tbsp all-purpose flour
- 3 tbsp cocoa powder
- ½ tsp baking powder
- ¼ tsp baking soda
- ¼ tsp salt
- ¼ cup softened butter
- ½ cup white sugar
- 1 large egg
- ½ tsp vanilla extract
- 6 oz buttermilk
- ¼ cup chocolate chips
- ¼ cup thick cream

Steps to Cook

1. Roll the dough balls. Place in the freezer for 30 minutes, or until frozen. Combine flour, baking powder, baking soda, salt and cocoa powder in a bowl. Set aside. Beat the butter and sugar in a bowl with an electric mixer. Add the egg, vanilla extract and mix until combined. Add the flour mixture and the butter milk in batches until incorporated.

2. Grease the mold to bite eggs. Place the pieces of cookie dough in the egg-biting pan. Pour the dough on top. Pour 1 cup of water. Cook under high pressure 12 minutes. Quick release Delete. Let cool completely in the pan. Eliminating them too soon will cause them to crumble. Use a knife to loosen. Prepare ganache. Add the thick cream and chocolate chips in a microwave safe container. Cook for 1 minute. Open and stir until chocolate and soft. Pour over the bites. Enjoy

Tastiest & healthiest...

Jamaican Cornmeal Porridge

Servings: 6

Calories: 424

Preparation time: 5 minutes

Cook time: 16 minutes

Ingredients	Steps to Cook

Ingredients

- 4 separate cups of water
- 1 cup of milk
- 1 cup fine yellow cornmeal
- 2 cinnamon sticks
- 3 pepper berries
- 1 teaspoon vanilla extract
- ½ teaspoon ground nutmeg
- ½ cup sweetened condensed milk

Steps to Cook

1. Add 3 cups of water and 1 cup of milk to the instant pot and stir. In a separate bowl, beat 1 cup of water and cornmeal until completely combined.

2. Add to the instant pot and whis. Add cinnamon sticks, pepper berries, vanilla extract and nutmeg.

3. Cover and cook on porridge for 6 minutes. Once the timer is turned off, allow it to release naturally for at least 10 minutes, then quickly release any remaining pressure.

4. Once done with natural release, open Instant Pot and beat to remove any lump. Add sweetened condensed milk to sweeten. Enjoy!!

Brownie

Servings: 3

Calories: 129

Preparation time: 5 minutes

Cook time: 8 minutes

Ingredients

- 2 large eggs
- 100 g of sugar
- 50 g of butter
- 70 g of flour
- 1 teaspoon of yeast coffee
- 25 g of pure cocoa
- 3 tablespoons filled with chopped almonds
- Vanilla aroma

Steps to Cook

1. Beat the eggs with the sugar and butter with the electric mixer until you get a little foam.
2. Incorporate the vanilla aroma.
3. Add the flour and cocoa and continue beating well.
4. When everything is integrated, add the almond and move with a spatula to finish mixing.
5. Pour into a pan that enters the pot, greased and floured.
6. Pour 2 fingers of water into the pot more or less, insert the mold. Cook for 8 minutes.

Bread Pudding

Servings: 8

Calories: 377

Preparation time: 5 minutes

Cook time: 15 minutes

Ingredients

- 4 eggs
- 1/2 liter milk
- 150 gr. bread from the day before
- 100 gr. sugar
- 1 piece lemon peel
- 1 cinnamon stick
- Liquid candy
- 2 tablespoons liquor (optional)
- cream for garnish

Steps to Cook

1. Put the caramel in the pan, and put it in the freezer. Heat the milk with the sugar, the lemon peel and the cinnamon. It can be heated in the microwave, and set aside before it starts to boil. Remove the lemon and cinnamon, and soak the bread in pieces.

2. Beat the eggs, and mix with the previous preparation. Whisk a little more, if you want to have the consistency of the smallest pieces of bread. Pour the preparation into the caramelized flan, cover and place it in the pot with three fingers of water and cook 15 minutes.

3. When time is over, remove the pan, and let the mold cool so that the pudding does not break. Unmold the pudding and serve it.

Conclusion

In this book, we have seen a lot about the instant pot. We've seen that cooking everything in a pot saves time and effort when it comes to cleaning, preparing, and controlling your food. It also means that everything is ready at the same time. You don't have to try to coordinate everything so that it is ready at the same time.

The instant pot will cook your food to perfection quickly and without constant monitoring. From hard-boiled eggs, your rice will be fluffy and perfect (it won't dry out or burn) and your stews will be tasty, tender and with the right consistency, also cookies, biscuits, etc., all is possible with instant pot.

Finally, we can say that instant pots have multiple uses and ways of cooking, which can make it the most used kitchen appliance in your home. Just remember that not all pots are created equal. So, some will have more functionality than others. To take advantage of them, you will have to research the different brands and models to decide which one best suit your needs.

CPSIA information can be obtained
at www.ICGtesting.com
Printed in the USA
LVHW061751050723
751493LV00026B/315